FACET BOOKS

BIBLICAL SERIES

FACET **fb** BOOKS

BIBLICAL SERIES — 8

John Reumann, General Editor

The Lord's Prayer

by JOACHIM JEREMIAS

translated by John Reumann

FORTRESS PRESS   PHILADELPHIA

This book is a translation of *Das Vater-Unser im Lichte der Neueren Forschung*, No. 50 in the series "Calwer Hefte," edited by Theodor Schlatter and published by Calwer Verlag, Stuttgart, in 1962. A different, briefer English version appeared in *The Expository Times*, Vol. lxxi, No. 5 (February, 1960), pp. 141-146 (published by T. & T. Clark, Edinburgh).

Lord's prayer

Library of Congress Catalog Card Number 64-11859

6973L63   Printed in U.S.A.   UB3008

Introduction

THE Lord's Prayer commands perennial interest—because we know it so little and because we know it so well. Word for word, few creations in all the history of literature have received so much attention, and probably no other prayer has wielded as much influence in the history of religious devotions. In part this is because it is the prayer, the only one, which the Lord of Christians, Jesus of Nazareth, enjoined on his disciples. In part it is because the prayer is terse in its phraseology but universal in the aspiration of its petitions. Partly too this prayer's unique position results from incessant usage, in church and without, and from our awareness that somehow we have never yet plumbed its depths.

But just because the Lord's Prayer is profound, we need ever new attempts to fathom its meaning for our day. Because it is familiar, we need to hear its contents restated in a way that can jab our prayers awake. Because it is remote, we face dangers in praying it today. It speaks of a "Father in heaven," and we live in a space age where "heaven" is a dubious concept and men have their own ideas about the "father-image." It hopes for "kingdom come," in a day when men see only this present materialistic age. In our affluent society this prayer seems to talk simply of "daily bread." It seems to seek immunity from temptation in a world where we know everything consists of shades of gray and where we are constantly faced with seducing lures. Precisely because this prayer seems twenty centuries thus removed from our thought world, we need a guide to lead us through its ancient landmarks, so that we may pray as Jesus first taught and encouraged his disciples to pray.

And when our guide undertakes to elucidate the Lord's Prayer "in the light of recent research" (such was the subtitle of Professor Jeremias' presentation in its German version), then doubtless interest quickens, for all of us know some of the exciting things which modern biblical research has done in peeling away certain barriers and accretions between our age and that of Jesus. At the same time there is probably trepidation as well as curiosity, for most of us are also aware of how traditional landmarks have been defaced or removed in the name of "modern research." For all Christians the Lord's Prayer is holy ground, and we may rightly wonder what recent research has done with this precious gift. Perhaps we shall not be too surprised if research, as it often seems to do, truncates the prayer we pray today and upsets some of our cherished notions about what it means. But perhaps we should be properly amazed—and grateful too—if this process of scholarly examination of the Lord's Prayer helps us to join in saying it with something of the meaning and freshness with which the first Christians prayed it. It would be gain if we could cut through some of the problems, both traditional and modern, to discover His meaning instead of ours.

There are and indeed always have been problems connected with the Lord's Prayer, and details which still puzzle New Testament scholars. Everyone knows, for example, that two different versions are found in the New Testament, one at Matthew 6 and the other in Luke 11, and that these two versions differ in content and length. These differences involve not just little words like "and" or "but," but the presence or omission of whole petitions. Anyone who alternates reading some modern English translation of the Bible (like the Revised Standard Version) with the King James Bible of 1611 knows further that there are differences in the Lucan version between the 1611 and the modern translations; differences are also uncovered if one thus examines the Matthean version. And as if this were not confusing enough, the fact of the matter is that many a churchgoer prays the Lord's Prayer Sunday after Sunday in a form which is neither that of Matthew nor of

Luke, using words which are not wholly those of the King James or the Revised Standard Versions but an "ecclesiastical formulation" which does not accord in every detail with any standard English Bible translation. In church, for example, we may say "forgive us our trespasses," though Matthew has "debts" and Luke "sins." It may be added by way of explanation, however, that Matthew 6:14-15 does use this word "trespasses" in a comment by Jesus attached to the prayer. Hesitation over "debts" and "trespasses" may still occur at ecumenical gatherings, accentuating diversity among Christians, but the old Federal Council of Churches once recommended liturgical use of the term "trespasses" for the sake of uniformity— a practice now widespread. And the idea of an ecclesiastical formulation of the Lord's Prayer will turn out to be considerably more biblical than most people suppose. As Professor Jeremias shows, our Matthean version is already "ecclesiastical," a product of the primitive Christian church and its devotional life.

Examples of other problems connected with the Lord's Prayer can easily be multiplied. In union churches in the "Dutch country" of eastern Pennsylvania it was long said that one of the chief distinguishing marks between the Reformed and the Lutheran congregations was that one said "Vater unser," and the other "Unser Vater"! To take a more significant illustration, it is not widely appreciated just how rare references to the Lord's Prayer actually are in Christian literature of the first four centuries. Apart from its presence in Matthew and Luke and in another first-century document called the *Didache*, there is nowhere any allusion to it in any second-century source; the Apologists do not even mention it by name! It is only about A.D. 350 that we get clear discussion of its contents. Why this "tunnel period," devoid of any open reference to such a precious treasure? Professor Jeremias has an answer which runs contrary to modern notions that our early Christian forefathers might have impressed pagans with the nobility of their religion by reciting the Lord's Prayer. When he argues (in good company with other recent scholars) that the Lord's Prayer in the ancient church was reserved for Christians only, and not recited with every Tom, Dick, and Harry, he is perhaps saying something as modern as (and pertinent to) the Supreme Court decision of 1963 on Bible reading and prayer in the public schools. For if the author of the *Didache,* or Matthew or Luke for that matter, were to behold our use of the Lord's Prayer in a mixed group of Christians and non–Christians, or our habit of "repeating together the Lord's Prayer" as a convenient device to close any and every meeting, might he not be shocked that we have moved so far from its original use?

To the investigation of such problems in the background and meaning of the Lord's Prayer, Professor Joachim Jeremias brings not only vast technical knowledge and scholarship, but also the ability to expound the Scriptures for the enrichment of Christian faith and life. For most students of the New Testament, and for readers of this series, Joachim Jeremias needs little introduction. He has been professor of New Testament Studies at Göttingen University in Germany since 1935. His special fields of interest have been the gospels (especially their Aramaic foundations), Jesus and his teachings, and baptism in the early church. His best known books, all of which have been translated into English, deal with the parables, the words of institution at the Last Supper, non-canonical sayings attributed to Jesus, and the relation of Jesus to the Gentiles. He has also produced definitive works on Jerusalem in Jesus' day and on the type of tombs and graves found near the Holy City in the time of Christ. His articles in learned journals have dealt especially with rabbinic backgrounds to the New Testament, and for the famed *Theologisches Wörterbuch* he has produced more than twenty-five articles, particularly on proper nouns of Semitic origin, including "Moses" and "Elijah," and also "gates of Hell" and "Servant of God." His presentation of the case for infant baptism as a practice in the early church has been part of the larger discussion in Europe and beyond, roused by Karl Barth's opposition to the practice today, and has led to a reply by Kurt Aland, another

New Testament scholar—to whom Professor Jeremias has in return replied with another small book!

The Sermon on the Mount, a brief essay by Dr. Jeremias on the origins and meaning of Matthew 5-7, has already appeared in this series of Facet Books, and since the Lord's Prayer in Matthew 6 is a part of the Sermon on the Mount, readers will find that some of the conclusions presented there about the Sermon must be utilized here to explain certain features of the Lord's Prayer. A number of emphases here stressed within the prayer have been further developed in some of the author's other recent writings and in his American lecture tour during the fall of 1963. Especially is this true of his views on the term *abba*, "father," as a keystone for the understanding of Jesus' message.

This emphasis on the word *abba* and its implications might be called an example of the "recent research" which Professor Jeremias has in mind as he explores the Lord's Prayer. "Recent research" means the scholarly, scientific study of the New Testament carried on particularly in the last three decades, as the literature cited by Professor Jeremias at the end of this book makes clear. These decades of scholarly work depend also in part on the solid results of work done in the previous half century, as some of the footnote references show. This research has gone on in a number of areas within New Testament studies, on all of which Dr. Jeremias draws to shape his conclusions.

For example there has been more than a century of critical work on the text of the New Testament. This has involved minute study of literally thousands of manuscripts in Greek and other languages, in an effort to ascertain the best and earliest text possible. Such work continues uninterruptedly as new documents are discovered and old evidence is more precisely assessed. Even since Professor Jeremias wrote this essay, a newly found copy of the Gospel of Luke, written between A.D. 175 and 225, and containing the Lord's Prayer in its usual Lucan form, has been published under the name of Papyrus Bodmer XIV, with the identifying number P^{75}. Another recently published papyrus dating from the third century A.D., from Antinoöpolis, a city in Egypt named by the Emperor Hadrian for his favorite friend Antinous who drowned in the Nile, contains most of the Lord's Prayer in its Matthean form. Such documents give us the two oldest copies of the Lord's Prayer and are typical of the sort of evidence which enables a scholar to draw his conclusions about the text.

Besides textual criticism there is the word study method as a tool in research. Professor Jeremias demonstrates its use as he treats the term *abba*, a theme which he has examined even further in an article in German. The same technique must be used with respect to "daily bread" in the Fourth Petition of the Lord's Prayer. We are not sure of the precise meaning of the Greek word *epioúsios*, conventionally rendered "daily." Everyone agrees that this rendering gets the sense as well as possible, but no one is completely sure about the derivation of the Greek word, nor do we have any other clear examples of its use in the whole of Greek literature. It has been widely assumed that one, if not two, such examples have been preserved from antiquity. However, a careful note by Professor Bruce Metzger of Princeton Theological Seminary recently pointed out that the one example must be conceded to have been misread, and the other is a question mark because the papyrus in which the word occurred was loaned to a friend by its owner and the friend seems to have mislaid it! This being the situation, Professor Jeremias has attempted a flanking maneuver. Balked in efforts to get at the precise sense of the Greek term, he has turned to a patristic reference to an Aramaic word in the *Gospel of the Nazarenes* to find a solution. Admittedly, not all who treat this Aramaic reference agree that Professor Jeremias' solution is correct (cf. note 21, below), but for the present this view may be said to provide the most satisfying solution, given the evidence available. Here too research continues. D. Y. Hadidian has recently tried to solve the mystery of the word *epioúsios* by use of certain Armenian manuscripts and their reading at II Maccabees 1:8; on this basis he suggests that the phrase in the Lord's Prayer means "bread of continuity"—a sense perhaps not completely alien to the idea of "bread for tomorrow," "bread of life," which Dr. Jeremias proposes.

Still another important area in research includes the actual usage of the Lord's Prayer by early Christians. They prayed it, but how, when, in what services? This area of investigation, of course, again involves text criticism, but it also draws in what we conventionally call "liturgics" and "patristics." The scholar must try to explain why some church fathers give variant clauses for portions of the Lord's Prayer. After all, we use the Lord's Prayer ourselves in varying forms for different occasions in public worship; we do not always pray the full "ecclesiastical form" together. In the Lutheran *Service Book and Hymnal,* for example, at Communion the minister says the prayer alone, with the congregation joining in to sing the closing doxology; and in the General Suffrages the leader of worship says the prayer through the Sixth Petition, the congregation responds with "But deliver us from evil," and there is no doxology. Even if we are unaccustomed to such variety in public use of the Lord's Prayer, surely all of us are familiar with the device of putting this prayer into our own words for private use, whatever may be the formal public wording that we use. Now if we thus employ the Lord's Prayer in varying forms, it should not surprise us that the ancient church did much the same thing, though we may be startled by Professor Jeremias' view that two forms were circulating already in the New Testament period, when Matthew and Luke wrote their gospels. All this perhaps suggests the necessity, by the way, for seeing liturgical study as basically integrated into biblical studies and church history in general. It is simply a truism today that no New Testament scholar can proceed far in his work without an awareness of the importance of worship in the primitive Christian community; but, conversely, he cannot always accept uncritically traditional notions of what ancient devotions were like. Studies along just such lines do exist on the Lord's Prayer. In 1891 Frederic Henry Chase, later the Bishop of Ely, published *The*

Lord's Prayer in the Early Church, and in 1955 the late T. W. Manson offered two lengthy articles in *Bulletin of the John Rylands Library*, which Professor Jeremias cites approvingly.

Source analysis and form criticism also play a part in the analysis of the two versions of the Lord's Prayer in Matthew and Luke; but there is one other area of New Testament study which deserves final note. That is the matter of Aramaic origins. It is commonly recognized that while our canonical gospels, so far as we know, were first composed in Greek, Aramaic sources do underlie them—and Aramaic was the Semitic language which Jesus himself spoke. Interest in Jesus' mother tongue characterizes much of Professor Jeremias' work, and this present essay is no exception. It should be noted, however, that his effort at reconstructing the prayer as originally spoken in Aramaic is no isolated attempt; a number of scholarly works have dealt with the same problem (cf. note 12, below). Again, while details in such efforts will continue to be debated, it may be said that there is rather wide agreement on many features in such Aramaic reconstructions. Related to these Aramaic origins is the fact that parallels to much of the Lord's Prayer (and to Jesus' teachings in general) exist in early Jewish sources; Jeremias, for example, draws on parallels from a prayer called the *Qaddish*. Readers interested in results of research in this area ought to consult the studies of Jewish scholars, in particular those of Isaac Abrahams or Claude G. Montefiore.

There are, of course, a number of long monographs in German on the Lord's Prayer; included in the list of literature cited by Jeremias at the end of this book are those of Paul Fiebig, Ernst Lohmeyer, and, from the Roman Catholic side, Heinz Schürmann. In English, readers ought to look up the treatments by A. M. Hunter, E. F. Scott, and C. W. F. Smith, plus the generally overlooked volume by A. R. George, *Communion with God in the New Testament*, which deals with prayer generally as well as the Lord's Prayer specifically. The study on the composition of the Lord's Prayer by the Rev. M. D. Goulder in *The Journal of Theological Studies* for

April, 1963, which reaches conclusions quite the reverse of many commentators—viz., that the Lord's Prayer does not go back to Jesus but was worked up by Matthew in light of certain precepts and examples recorded in Mark, and was then in turn abbreviated and amended by Luke—does not seem to be aware of Professor Jeremias' careful study, nor for that matter of any of the monographs in German. Bibliographical details on these and all other titles mentioned in this Introduction are given at the end of the book in the section headed "For Further Reading."

Professor Jeremias' study on the Lord's Prayer has grown in its presentation over the years. Given as a lecture at Cambridge University in May, 1957, the essay first appeared in print in English, translated anonymously, under the title "The Lord's Prayer in Modern Research," in *The Expository Times*, Vol. 1xxi, No. 5 (Feb., 1960), pp. 141-146 (published by T. & T. Clark, Edinburgh, by whose kind permission use has been made of it in preparing this volume for Facet Books). In 1962 a greatly expanded form of the essay was published in German, *Das Vater-Unser im Lichte der Neueren Forschung* ("Calwer Hefte," No. 50; Stuttgart: Calwer Verlag). In order to provide the fuller insights of this more recent version, what amounts to a fresh translation from the German has been made by the General Editor, though the allusions particularly pertinent for readers in English-speaking countries and as much phraseology as possible from the version in *The Expository Times* have been preserved. The composite, revised translation appears now with Professor Jeremias' approval; at a few points expansions have been made by him to clarify possible ambiguities. The Revised Standard Version of the Bible has been used throughout except where the author provides a loose paraphrase of the original or offers his own version of a reconstructed Aramaic text.

Lutheran Theological Seminary   JOHN REUMANN
Philadelphia
October, 1963

Contents

The Lord's Prayer

in standard English translations

MATTHEW 6:9-13

THE KING JAMES VERSION (1611)

9 Our Father which art in heaven,
Hallowed be thy name.
10 Thy kingdom come.
Thy will be done in earth,
    as *it is* in heaven.
11 Give us this day our daily bread.
12 And forgive us our debts,
    as we forgive our debtors.

13 And lead us not into temptation,
    but deliver us from evil:
For thine is the kingdom, and the
    power, and the glory, for ever. Amen.

THE REVISED STANDARD VERSION (1946)

9 Our Father who art in heaven,
Hallowed be thy name.
10 Thy kingdom come.
Thy will be done,
    On earth as it is heaven.
11 Give us this day our daily bread;*
12 And forgive us our debts,
    As we also have forgiven our debtors;

13 And lead us not into temptation,
    But deliver us from evil.†

The Lord's Prayer

in standard English translations

LUKE 11:2-4

THE KING JAMES VERSION (1611)

2 Our Father which art in heaven,
Hallowed be thy name.
Thy kingdom come.
Thy will be done, as in heaven,
  so in earth.
3 Give us day by day our daily bread.
4 And forgive us our sins;
    for we also forgive every one
      that is indebted to us.
And lead us not into temptation;
    but deliver us from evil.

THE REVISED STANDARD VERSION (1946)

2 Father,
  hallowed be thy name.
  Thy kingdom come.

3 Give us each day our daily bread;*
4 and forgive us our sins,
  for we ourselves forgive every
    one who is indebted to us;
  and lead us not into temptation.

* Or *our bread for the morrow*. † Or *the evil one*. Other authorities, some ancient, add, in some form, *For thine is the kingdom and the power and the glory, for ever. Amen.*

THE LORD'S PRAYER IN THE
ANCIENT CHURCH

DURING the time of Lent and Easter in the year
A.D. 350, a Jerusalem presbyter, Cyril by name, who was con-
secrated as bishop a year later, presented his celebrated twenty-
four Catechetical Lectures in the Church of the Holy Sepul-
cher. These lectures, which have been preserved for us through
the shorthand notes of one of Cyril's hearers,[1] fall into two
parts. Those in the first part prepared the candidates for the
baptism which they were to receive on Easter Eve. The focal
point of these prebaptismal lectures was the exposition of the
confession of faith, the Jerusalem Creed. The last five lectures,
however, were presented during Easter week. These postbap-
tismal lectures instructed the newly baptized about the sacraments which they had received. For this reason they were
called "mystagogical catechetical lectures," that is, lectures
which introduced the hearers to the "mysteries" or sacraments
of the Christian faith. In the last of these mystagogical lectures, Cyril explains for his hearers the liturgy of the Mass, or
Service of Holy Communion, especially the prayers which
are spoken there. Among these is the Lord's Prayer.

[1] [The Greek text and an English translation are conveniently given
in *St. Cyril of Jerusalem's Lectures on the Christian Sacraments*, ed.
F. L. Cross ("Texts for Students," No. 51; London: SPCK, 1951), or,
translation alone, in *Cyril of Jerusalem and Nemesius of Emesa*, ed. William Telfer ("The Library of Christian Classics," Volume IV; Philadelphia: Westminster, 1955).—EDITOR.]

This final (twenty-fourth) Catechetical Lecture by Cyril of Jerusalem is our earliest proof for the fact that the Lord's Prayer was regularly employed in the Service. The position in the Service where the Lord's Prayer was prayed is to be noted: it came immediately before the Communion. As a constituent part of the Communion liturgy, the Lord's Prayer belonged to that portion of the Service in which only those who were baptized were permitted to participate, i.e., it belonged to the so-called *missa fidelium* or "Service for the baptized." The late Professor T. W. Manson[2] has shown that this leads to the conclusion that knowledge of the Lord's Prayer and the privilege to use it were reserved for the full members of the church.

What we have demonstrated for Jerusalem holds for the ancient church as a whole. Everywhere the Lord's Prayer was a constituent part of the celebration of the Lord's Supper, and everywhere the Lord's Prayer, together with the creed, belonged to those items in which the candidates for baptism were instructed either just before baptism or, as we saw in the case of Cyril, in the days directly after baptism. Petition by petition, the Lord's Prayer was elucidated, and then the whole recapitulated in an address to the converts. Thus those seeking baptism or those newly baptized learned the Lord's Prayer by heart. They were allowed to join in praying it for the first time in their first Service of Holy Communion, which was attached to the rite of their baptism. Henceforth they prayed it daily, and it formed a token of their identification as Christians. Because the privilege of praying the Lord's Prayer was limited to the baptized members of the church, it was called the "prayer of believers."

The connection of the Lord's Prayer with baptism can be traced back to early times. In the beginning of the second century, we find a variant to Luke 11:2 which reads: "Thy Holy Spirit come upon us and cleanse us." The heretic Marcion (about A.D. 140) had this instead of the first petition. His

[2] T. W. Manson, "The Lord's Prayer," *Bulletin of the John Rylands Library*, XXXVIII (1955-56), Part 1, pp. 99-113, and Part 2, pp. 436-48.

wording of the Lord's Prayer seems to have been as follows: "Father, Thy Holy Spirit come upon us and cleanse us. Thy kingdom come. Thy bread for the morrow give us day by day. And forgive us our sins, for we also forgive everyone who is indebted to us. And do not allow us to be led into temptation." Two of the Greek minuscule manuscripts (numbers 162, 700) and two late church fathers (Gregory of Nyssa † 394, and Maximus Confessor † 662) have the petition for the Holy Spirit instead of the second petition. It is quite improbable that the petition for the Holy Spirit should be the original text; its attestation is much too weak. From where, then, does this petition originate? We know that it was an old baptismal prayer, and we may conclude that it was added to the Lord's Prayer when this was used at the baptismal ceremony. One may compare the fact that the Marcionite version of the Prayer, quoted above, has, in the petition for bread, "Thy bread." This is probably an allusion to the Lord's Supper; thus Marcion has both sacraments in view, baptism in this first petition and the Lord's Supper, which followed baptism, in his phrase "Thy bread."

But we must go even one step further back. The connection of the Lord's Prayer with baptism which we have found already in the first part of the second century can be traced back even into the first century. It is true that at first glance, we seem to get a completely different picture when we turn to the *Didache*, or *Teaching of the Twelve Apostles*. This document is the oldest "church order," the basic part of which is dated by its most recent commentator, perhaps somewhat too optimistically, as early as A.D. 50-70,[3] but which in all likelihood does nonetheless belong in the first Christian century. In the *Didache* (8:2), the Lord's Prayer is cited, word for word, introduced by the admonition, "Do not pray as the hypocrites; but as the Lord commanded in his gospel, thus pray ye." The Prayer concludes with a doxology consisting of two terms, "for thine is the power and the glory for ever."

[3] Jean-Paul Audet, *La Didachè: Instructions des Apôtres* (Paris: Gabalda, 1958), p. 219.

There then follows (in 8:3) the advice, "Three times a day, pray thus." Here, in the earliest period, regular use of the Lord's Prayer is therefore presupposed, though without any apparent connection with the sacraments. Yet this impression is false. The matter becomes clear if one notes the context in which the Lord's Prayer stands in the *Didache*.[4] The *Didache* begins with instruction in the "Two Ways," the Way of Life and the Way of Death (chapters 1-6); this teaching no doubt belonged to the instruction of candidates for baptism. Chapter 7 treats baptism; and then begin the sections which are important for those who are baptized: fasting and prayer (including the Lord's Prayer) are treated in chapter 8, the Lord's Supper in chapters 9-10, and church organization and church discipline in chapters 11-15. For us it is important to note that the Lord's Prayer and the Lord's Supper follow upon baptism. Thereby the point we made at the beginning is corroborated: the Lord's Prayer was intended in the early church—beginning already in the first century, as we can now add—only for those who were full members of the church.

All this leads to a very important result which, again, T. W. Manson has pointed out most lucidly.[5] Whereas nowadays the Lord's Prayer is understood as a common property of all people, it was otherwise in the earliest times. As one of the most holy treasures of the church, the Lord's Prayer, together with the Lord's Supper, was reserved for full members, and it was not disclosed to those who stood outside. It was a privilege to be allowed to pray it. How great was the reverence and awe which surrounded it is best seen by the introductory formulae found both in the liturgies of the East and in those of the West. In the East, in the so-called Liturgy of St. John Chrysostom, which even today is still the usual form of

[4] Alfred Seeberg, "Die vierte Bitte des Vaterunsers" (Rostock: Rats- und Universitäts-Buchdruckerei, 1914), pp. 13-14, reprinted in *D. Alfred Seeberg, Worte des Gedächtnisses an die Heimgegangenen und Arbeiten aus seinem Nachlass*, ed. Reinhold Seeberg (Leipzig: A. Deichertsche Verlagsbuchhandlung, 1916), pp. 69-82; T. W. Manson, "The Lord's Prayer," *op. cit.*, pp. 101-02.

[5] *Ibid.*, pp. 101-02.

the mass among the Greek and Russian Orthodox, the priest prays, at the introduction of the Lord's Prayer, "And make us worthy, O Lord, that we joyously and without presumption may make bold to invoke Thee, the heavenly God, as Father, and to say: Our Father." The formula in the Roman mass in the West is similar: "We make bold to say [*audemus dicere*]: Our Father."

This awesome reverence before the Lord's Prayer was a reality in the ancient church, which, unfortunately, has been lost to us today for the most part. That should disquiet us. We ought therefore to ask ourselves whether we can again discover why the early church surrounded the Lord's Prayer with such reverence, so that they said, "We make bold to say, Our Father." Perhaps we may regain an inkling of the basis for this awe if, with the aid of the results of recent New Testament research, we try to discover, as best we can, how Jesus himself meant the words of the Lord's Prayer.

THE EARLIEST TEXT OF THE
LORD'S PRAYER

W̲E must first clear up a preliminary question, namely that of the earliest text of the Lord's Prayer. The Lord's Prayer has been handed down to us at two places in the New Testament, in Matthew as part of the Sermon on the Mount (Matt. 6:9-13), and in Luke in chapter 11 (Luke 11:2-4). Before trying to consider the original meaning of the petitions of the Prayer, we must face the strange fact that the two evangelists, Matthew and Luke, transmit it in slightly different wordings. It is true that in the King James Version the differences are limited, the main divergence being that in Luke the doxology is absent, i.e., the concluding words: "For thine is the kingdom, and the power, and the glory, for ever." Likewise in the older editions of the Luther Bible in German the two versions agree with one another, save for trivial variations and the absence of the doxology in Luke. But as a matter of fact, the divergences are greater than this. In the Revised Standard Version or in the New English Bible translation, just as in the newly revised Luther Bible or in the *Zürcherbibel*,[6] we read a form of the Lord's Prayer at Luke 11:2-4 which is briefer than that found in Matthew.

It is well known that in the last one hundred and twenty

[6] [The Zürich Bible was originally the work of the Reformers Ulrich Zwingli and Leo Jud. Like the Luther Bible, it has often been revised, notably in 1907-35 by a commission.—EDITOR.]

years research into the oldest text-form of the New Testament
has gone forward with great energy, first in Germany, and
then in England, and in the last decades also in America, and
admirable results have been achieved in recovering the oldest
text. This work was triggered by the discovery of numerous
manuscripts of the New Testament, often very ancient ones.
In 1961 the number of New Testament manuscripts in Greek
alone totaled 4,916. By comparing and classifying these manuscripts, scholars have succeeded in working out an earlier text
than that which the King James translators or Luther pos-
sessed. While for the 1611 translators or for Luther the text-
form was available much as it had been developed at the end
of the fourth century in the Byzantine church, we today know
the text of approximately the second century. One can say,
without exaggeration, that this chapter in research is essen-
tially concluded and that we today have attained the best
possible Greek text of the New Testament. With regard to
the Lord's Prayer, the results are as follows: At the time
when the gospels of Matthew and of Luke were being composed (about A.D. 75-85) the Lord's Prayer was being transmitted in two forms which agreed with each other in essentials,
but which differed in the fact that the one was longer than
the other. The longer form appears in Matthew 6:9-13 and
also, with insignificant variations, in the *Didache*, at 8:2; the
briefer form appears at Luke 11:2-4.

While the Matthean version agrees with that form which
is familiar to us, a form of the Prayer with seven petitions
(only the doxology is lacking in Matthew[7]), the Lucan version
has only five petitions according to the oldest manuscripts.
It runs:

> Father,
> Hallowed be thy name.
> Thy kingdom come.
> Give us each day our bread for tomorrow.
> And forgive us our sins, for we also forgive
>   everyone who is indebted to us.
> and let us not fall into temptation.

[7] On the doxology, see further on pp. 31-32.

7

Two questions now arise. (1) How is it that about the year A.D. 75 the Lord's Prayer was being transmitted and prayed in two forms which diverged from one another? And (2), which of the two forms is to be regarded as the original?

THE TWO FORMS

The answer to the first question, namely, how it is to be explained that the Lord's Prayer was transmitted in two forms, emerges when we observe the context in which the Lord's Prayer occurs in Matthew and Luke. In both cases the Lord's Prayer occurs with words of Jesus which treat prayer.

In Matthew we read, in the section 6:1-18, a discussion which opposes the type of piety practiced in the lay circles which formed the Pharisaic movement. The Lord reproves the fact that they offer their alms (6:2-4) and their prayers (6:5-6) and conduct their fasts (6:16-18) publicly for show and thus use them to serve their craving for approval and to feed their own self-conceit. In contrast he demands of his disciples that their almsgiving and prayer and fasting shall take place in secret, so that only God beholds it. The three units are symmetrically constructed: in each instance false and right conduct are contrasted with each other through two "when"–clauses. But the middle unit, which deals with prayer (6:5-6), is expanded through three further words of Jesus about prayer, so that the following structure arose: (a) The foundation was provided by the admonition of Jesus that his disciples were not to be like the Pharisees who arrange things so that they find themselves in the midst of the tumult of the market place when trumpet blasts from the Temple announce the hour of prayer, with the result that, evidently to their complete surprise, they have to pray amid the throng of men. No, Jesus' disciples are to pray behind closed doors, even, if need be, in so worldly a place as the storeroom (Greek, *tamiéion;* RSV, "your room"; 6:5-6). (b) To this there is joined Jesus' admonition not to "heap up empty phrases as the Gentiles do." As children of the heavenly Father, his disciples do not need to employ "many words" (6:7-8). (c)

The Lord's Prayer follows as an example of brief prayer (6: 9-13). As a matter of fact, this prayer from the Lord is distinguished from most prayers in late Judaism by its brevity. (d) Emphatic in its position at the end of this middle section is a saying of Jesus about inner disposition in prayer, a saying which connects with the petition on forgiveness: only he who is himself ready to forgive has the right to petition God for forgiveness (6:14-15). We thus have before us in Matthew 6:5-15 a catechism on prayer, put together from words of Jesus, a catechism which would be employed in the instruction of the newly baptized.

In Luke, too, the Lord's Prayer occurs in such a catechism on prayer (Luke 11:1-13). This indicates how important the primitive church considered the instruction of its members in the right kind of prayer. In Luke, however, the catechism on prayer is of a very different sort from that found in Matthew. But it too falls into four parts: (a) There is prefixed a picture of the Lord at prayer as a prototype for all Christian prayer, and the request of the disciples, "Lord, teach us to pray" (11:1). Jesus fulfills this request with the Lord's Prayer (11: 2-4). (b) The parable about the man who knocks on his friend's door at midnight is added here. In its present context it presents an admonition to persist in prayer, even if one's prayer is not heard immediately (11:5-8). (c) The same admonition then follows in imperative form: "Ask, and it will be given you" (11:9-10). (d) The conclusion is formed by the picture of the father who "gives good gifts" to his children (11:11-13).

The differences in these two primers on prayer are to be explained by the fact that they are directed at very different groups of people. The Matthean catechism on prayer is addressed to people who have learned to pray in childhood but whose prayer stands in danger of becoming a routine. The Lucan catechism on prayer, on the other hand, is addressed to people who must for the first time learn to pray and whose courage to pray must be roused. It is clear that Matthew is transmitting to us instruction on prayer directed at Jewish-

Christians, Luke at Gentile-Christians. About A.D. 75, therefore, the Lord's Prayer was a fixed element in instructions on prayer in all Christendom, in the Jewish–Christian as well as in the Gentile-Christian church. Both churches, different as their situations were, were at one on this point: that a Christian learned, from the Lord's Prayer, how to pray.

For our question then of how it is to be explained that in Matthew and Luke we find two forms of the Lord's Prayer which vary from each other, the conclusion is that the variations can in no case be traced back to the caprice of the evangelists—no author would have dared to make such alteration in the Prayer on his own—but rather that the variations are to be seen within a broader context: we have before us the wording for the Prayer from two churches, that is, different liturgical wordings of the Lord's Prayer. Each of the evangelists transmits to us the wording of the Lord's Prayer as it was prayed in his church at that time.

THE ORIGINAL FORM

Now we can deal with the second question: which of the two forms is to be regarded as the original?

If we compare the two texts carefully, the most striking divergence is the difference in length. The Lucan form (see p. 7) is shorter than that of Matthew at three places. First, the invocation is shorter. Luke says only "Father," or properly "dear Father," in Greek *páter*, in Aramaic *abba*, whereas Matthew says, according to the pious and reverent form of Palestinian invocation, "Our Father who art in heaven." Second, whereas Matthew and Luke agree in the first two petitions—the "Thou-petitions" ("Hallowed be thy name, thy kingdom come")—there follows in Matthew a third "Thou-petition": "Thy will be done in earth, as it is in heaven." Third, in Matthew the last of the following "We-petitions" has an antithesis. Luke has only: "And let us not fall into temptation," but Matthew adds: "but deliver us from evil."

Now, if we ask which form is the original—the longer form of Matthew or the shorter form of Luke—the decisive observation, which has not yet been mentioned, is the following: the shorter form of Luke is completely contained in the longer form of Matthew. This makes it very probable that the Matthean form is an expanded one, for according to all that we know about the tendency of liturgical texts to conform to certain laws in their transmission, in a case where the shorter version is contained in the longer one, the shorter text is to be regarded as original. No one would have dared to shorten a sacred text like the Lord's Prayer and to leave out two petitions if they had formed part of the original tradition. On the contrary, the reverse is amply attested, that in the early period, before wordings were fixed, liturgical texts were elaborated, expanded, and enriched. This conclusion, that the Matthean version represents an expansion, is confirmed by three supplementary observations. First, the three expansions which we find in Matthew, as compared with Luke, are always found toward the end of a section of the prayer—the first at the end of the address, the second at the end of the "Thou-petitions," the third at the end of the "We-petitions." This again is exactly in accordance with what we find elsewhere in the growth of liturgical texts; they show a proclivity for sonorous expansions at the end.

Second, it is of further significance that in Matthew the stylistic structure is more consistently carried through. Three "Thou-petitions" in Matthew correspond to the three "We-petitions" (the sixth and seventh petitions in Matthew were regarded as one petition). The third "We-petition," which in Luke seems abrupt because of its brevity, is in Matthew assimilated to the first two "We-petitions." To spell this out, the first two "We-petitions" show a parallelism:

> Our bread for tomorrow / give us today.[8]
> Do Thou forgive us / as we forgive.

In Luke, however, the third "We-petition" is shorter, apparently intentionally:

> And lead us not into temptation.

[8] On this two-part (or two half-lines) division of the petition for daily bread, see pp. 13, 17 and 23.

But Matthew offers a parallelism here too:

And lead us not into temptation / but deliver us from evil.

This endeavor to produce parallelism in lines (*parallelismus membrorum*) is a characteristic of liturgical tradition. One can see the point especially well if one compares the various versions of the words of institution at the Lord's Supper.[9]

Third, a final point in favor of the originality of the Lucan version is the reappearance of the brief form of address "dear Father" (*abba*) in the prayers of the earliest Christians, as we see from Romans 8:15 and Galatians 4:6. Matthew has a sonorous address, "Our Father who art in heaven," such as corresponded to pious Jewish–Palestinian custom. We shall see that the simple *abba* was a unique note in Jesus' own prayers. Thus we must conclude that this plain *abba* was the original address.

All these observations lead us, then, in the same direction. The common substance of both texts, which is identical with its Lucan form, is the oldest text. The Gentile–Christian church has handed down the Lord's Prayer without change, whereas the Jewish–Christian church, which lived in a world of rich liturgical tradition and used a variety of prayer forms, has enriched the Lord's Prayer liturgically. Because the form transmitted by Matthew was the more richly elaborated one, it soon permeated the whole church; we saw above[10] that the *Didache* presents this form too.

Of course, we must be cautious with our conclusions. The possibility remains that Jesus himself spoke the "Our Father" on different occasions in a slightly differing form, a shorter one and a longer one. But perhaps it would be safer to say that the shorter Lucan form is in all probability the oldest one, whereas Matthew gives us the earliest evidence that the Lord's Prayer was used liturgically in worship. In any case, the chief thing is that both texts agree in the decisive elements.

Nonetheless the question about the original form of the

[9] [Cf. J. Jeremias, *The Eucharistic Words of Jesus* (Oxford: Basil Blackwell, and New York: Macmillan, 1955).—EDITOR.]

[10] *Supra*, p. 7.

Lord's Prayer is still not completely answered. We have thus far directed our attention only to the varying lengths of the two versions. But in the lines where they share a common wording these versions also exhibit certain—admittedly, not very significant—variations, specifically in the second part, the "We-petitions." To these differences we now turn briefly.

The first "We-petition," for daily bread, reads in Matthew, "Give us this day our bread for the morrow." As we shall see later, the contrast, "this day—for the morrow," sets the whole tone for the verse. In Luke, on the other hand, it reads, "give us each day our bread for the morrow." Here the term "this day" is expanded into "each day"; the petition is thereby broadened into a generalized saying, with the consequence that the antithesis "this day—for the morrow" drops out. Moreover, in Luke the Greek word for "give" now had to be expressed with the present imperative (*didou,* literally "keep on giving!"), whereas elsewhere throughout the Prayer the aorist imperative is used, which denotes a single action. Matthew also has the aorist imperative in this petition: *dos,* "give!" From all this it may be concluded that the Matthean form of the petition for daily bread is the older one.

In the second "We-petition," for forgiveness, Matthew has "Forgive us our debts," while Luke has "Forgive us our sins." Now it was a peculiarity of Jesus' mother tongue, Aramaic, that the word *hobha* was used for "sin," though it properly meant a debt, "money owed." Matthew translates the word quite literally with "debts," *opheilēmata,* a word which is not usual in Greek for "sin"; this enables one to see that the Lord's Prayer goes back to an Aramaic wording. In the Lucan version, the word "debts" is represented by the usual Greek word for "sins," *hamartíai;* but the wording in the next clause ("for we ourselves forgive everyone who is *indebted* to us") makes it evident that in the initial clause "debts" had originally appeared. In this case, too, Matthew therefore has the older wording.

The same picture results when one focuses attention on yet a final variation in wording. We read in Matthew (literally translated), "as we also have forgiven [*aphêkamen*] our debtors," while in Luke we read, "for we also ourselves forgive [*aphíomen*] everyone who is indebted to us." When we ask which formulation is the older, the past tense in Matthew or the present tense form in Luke, it is readily seen that Matthew has the more difficult form, and in such cases the more difficult form is to be regarded as the more original. Matthew's is the more difficult form, because his wording ("as we have forgiven") could lead to the mistaken impression that our forgiving must not only precede forgiveness on God's part, but also that it provides the standard for God's forgiving us: "forgive us thus, as we have forgiven." In actuality, however, there lies behind Matthew's past tense form what is called in Semitic grammar a *perfectum praesens,* a "present perfect," which refers to an action occurring here and now. The correct translation of the Matthean form would therefore run, "as we also herewith forgive our debtors." By its choice of the present tense form, Luke's version was intended to exclude a misunderstanding among Greek-speaking Christians, since it says (and this catches the sense): "for we also ourselves forgive everyone who is indebted to us." Moreover, in the Lucan form, the petition on forgiveness is broadened by the addition of the word "everyone," which represents a sharpening of the meaning, in that it permits no exceptions in our forgiving.

Comparison of the wording of the two forms of the Lord's Prayer therefore shows that, over against Matthew, the Lucan form has been assimilated at several points to Greek linguistic usage. Viewed as a whole, our results may be summarized thus: the Lucan version has preserved the oldest form with respect to *length,* but the Matthean text is more original with regard to *wording.*

In our consideration of the petition for forgiveness, we have just observed that the Matthean phrase "our debts" enables one to see that the Lord's Prayer, which is of course preserved for us only in Greek, goes back to an original Aramaic version. As we shall see later,[11] this observation is confirmed by the

[11] *Infra,* p. 21.

fact that the two "Thou-petitions" relate to an Aramaic prayer, the *Qaddish*. When one attempts to put the Lord's Prayer back into Aramaic, Jesus' mother tongue, the conclusion begins to emerge that stylistically it continues the tradition of the liturgical language of the Psalter. Even the person who brings no knowledge of the Semitic languages to his reading of the following attempt at retranslation can easily spot the characteristic features of this solemn language. We should note three features especially: parallelism, the two-beat rhythm, and the rhyme in lines two and four, which is scarcely accidental. The Lord's Prayer in Jesus' tongue sounded something like this (the accents designate the two-beat rhythm)[12]:

> *'Abbâ'*
> *yithqaddásh shᵉmákh / tethé malkhuthákh*
> *lahmán dᵉlimhár / habh lán yoma' dhén*
> *ushᵉbhoq lán hobháin / kᵉdhishᵉbháqnan lᵉhayyabháin*
> *wᵉla' thaʻelínnan lᵉnisyón.*

---

[12] On the problem of the original Aramaic form and attempts at retranslation of the Lord's Prayer into Aramaic, cf. C. C. Torrey, "The Translations made from the Original Aramaic Gospels," in *Studies in the History of Religions presented to Crawford Howell Toy by Pupils, Colleagues and Friends* (New York: Macmillan, 1912), pp. 309-17; *The Four Gospels* (New York: Harper, 1933), p. 292; E. Littmann, "Torreys Buch über die vier Evangelien," in *Zeitschrift für die Neutestamentliche Wissenschaft*, XXXIV (1935), 20-34, especially pp. 29-30; C. F. Burney, *The Poetry of Our Lord* (Oxford: Clarendon Press, 1925), pp. 112-13; G. Dalman, *Die Worte Jesu mit Berücksichtigung des nachkanonischen jüdischen Schrifttums und der aramäischen Sprache erörtert* (Leipzig: J. C. Hinrichs'sche Buchhandlung, ²1930), Band I, pp. 283-365 [the "Anhang" on "Das Vaterunser" does not appear in the first German edition of 1898, nor in the English translation by D. M. Kay, *The Words of Jesus* (Edinburgh: T. & T. Clark, 1902)]; and K. G. Kuhn, *Achtzehngebet und Vaterunser und der Reim* ("Wissenschaftliche Untersuchungen zum Neuen Testament," No. 1; Tübingen: J. C. B. Mohr, 1950), pp. 32-33.

THE MEANING OF THE LORD'S PRAYER

Having considered what can be said about the original wording, we are prepared to face the main question. What was, as far as we can judge, the original meaning?

Luke reports that Jesus gave the Lord's Prayer to his disciples on a quite specific occasion.

> He was praying in a certain place, and when he ceased, one of his disciples said to him, "Lord, teach us to pray, as John taught his disciples." (11:1)

That the unnamed disciple appealed to the example of John the Baptist is important for our understanding of the Lord's Prayer, since we know that at the time of Jesus individual religious groups were marked by their own prayer customs and forms. This was true of the Pharisees, the Essenes, and, as we perceive from Luke 11:1, the disciples of John as well. A particular custom in prayer expressed the particular relationship with God which bound the individuals together. The request at Luke 11:1 therefore shows that Jesus' disciples recognized themselves as a community and that they requested of Jesus a prayer which would bind them together and identify them, in that it would bring to expression their chief concern. As a matter of fact, the Lord's Prayer is the clearest and, in spite of its terseness, the most comprehensive summary of Jesus' proclamation which we possess. When the Lord's Prayer was given to the disciples, prayer in Jesus' name began (John 14:13-14, 15:16, 16:23).[13]

[13] K. H. Rengstorf, *Das Evangelium nach Lukas* ("Das Neue Testament Deutsch," 3; Göttingen: Vandenhoeck und Ruprecht, 8¹1958), p. 144.

The structure of the Lord's Prayer is simple and transparent. We present once again what is presumably the oldest wording (following the short form according to Luke, but where there are minor variations of wording that of Matthew):

> Dear Father,
> Hallowed be thy name,
> Thy kingdom come,
> Our bread for tomorrow / give us today,
> And forgive us our debts / as we also herewith forgive our debtors,
> And let us not fall into temptation.

The structure of the Lord's Prayer then consists of: (1) the address; (2) two "Thou-petitions" in parallel (in Matthew, three); (3) two "We-petitions" in parallel, both forming, as we shall see, an antithesis; (4) the concluding request. We also observe what seems to be an apparently insignificant point: while the two "Thou-petitions" stand side-by-side without any "and," the two parallel "We-petitions" are connected by an "and."

THE ADDRESS "DEAR FATHER" (ABBA)

When we trace back to its earliest beginnings the history of the invocation of God as father, we have the feeling of descending into a mine in which new and unexpected treasures are disclosed one after another. It is surprising to see that already in the ancient Orient, as early as the third and second millennia B.C., we find the deity addressed as father. We find this title for the first time in Sumerian prayers, long before the time of Moses and the prophets, and there already the word "father" does not merely refer to the deity as procreator and ancestor of the king and of the people and as powerful lord, but it also has quite another significance: it is used for the "merciful, gracious father, in whose hand the life of the whole land lies" (a hymn from Ur to the moon god Sin).[14]

---

[14] ["Hymn to the Moon–God," in *Ancient Near Eastern Texts relating to the Old Testament*, ed. James B. Pritchard (Princeton University Press, 1950), p. 385, cf. lines 2-9 and 13.—EDITOR.]

For Orientals, the word "father," as applied to God, thus encompasses, from earliest times, something of what the word "mother" signifies among us.

When we turn to the Old Testament, we find that God is only seldom spoken of as father—in fact only on fourteen occasions, but all these are important. God is Israel's father, but now not mythologically as procreator or ancestor, but as the one who elected, delivered, and saved his people Israel by mighty deeds in history. This designation of God as father in the Old Testament comes to full fruition, however, in the message of the prophets. God is Israel's father. But the prophets must make constant accusation against God's people that Israel has not given God the honor which a son should give to his father.

> A son honors his father,
>   and a servant his master.
> If then I am a father,
>   where is my honor?
> And if I am a master,
>   where is my fear?
>   says the Lord of hosts.
>   (Mal. 1:6; cf. Deut. 32:5-6; Jer. 3:19-20)

And Israel's answer to this rebuke is a confession of sin and the ever-reiterated cry, *Abhinu atta*, "Thou art our father" (Isa. 63:15-16, 64:7-8; Jer. 3:4). And God's reply to this cry is mercy beyond all understanding:

> "Is Ephraim my dear son?
>   Is he my darling child? . . .
> Therefore my heart yearns for him;
> I will surely have mercy on him,
>   says the Lord." (Jer. 31:20)

Can there be any deeper dimension to the term "father" than this compulsive, forgiving mercy which is beyond comprehension?

When we turn to Jesus' preaching, the answer must be:

Yes, here there is something quite new, absolutely new—the word *abba*. From the prayer in Gethsemane, Mark 14:36, we learn that Jesus addressed God with this word, and this point is confirmed not only by Romans 8:15 and Galatians 4:6, but also by the striking oscillation of the forms for the vocative "O father" in the Greek text of the gospels, an oscillation which is to be explained only through the fact that the Aramaic term *abba* lies behind all such passages.[15] With the help of my assistants I have examined the prayer literature of Late Judaism—a large, rich literature, all too little explored. The result of this examination was that in no place in this immense literature is this invocation of God as *abba* to be found. How is this to be explained? The church fathers Chrysostom, Theodor of Mopsuestia, and Theodoret of Cyrrhus who originated from Antioch (where the populace spoke the West Syrian dialect of Aramaic) and who probably had Aramaic-speaking nurses, testify unanimously that *abba* was the address of the small child to his father. And the Talmud confirms this when it says: "When a child experiences the taste of wheat [i.e., when it is weaned], it learns to say *abba* and *imma* ["dear father" and "dear mother"]."[16] *Abba* and *imma* are thus the first sounds which the child stammers. *Abba* was an everyday word, a homely family-word, a secular word, the tender address of the child to its father: "Dear father." No Jew would

[15] [In the gospels, where Jesus addresses God as father, the form of the Greek varies curiously. Sometimes the vocative case is used, as one would expect (in Greek, *páter;* Matt. 11:25; Luke 11:2, 23:34, 46; John 11:41, 12:27-28, 17:1, 5), at times with the first person singular suffix, "O my father" (in Greek, *páter mou;* Matt. 26:39, 42). On other occasions, however, the nominative form is used as a vocative, with the article, *ho patêr* (Matt. 11:26, Mark 14:36; cf. Rom. 8:15, Gal. 4:6), or without it (John 17:11, 21, 24, 25). The assumption that *abba* in Aramaic stands behind all these varying Greek forms is advanced by Gerhard Kittel in the *Theologisches Wörterbuch zum Neuen Testament*, Vol. I (Stuttgart, 1933), p. 5, lines 24-28; cf. also Gottlob Schrenk's article on *patêr* in the *Wörterbuch*, Vol. V (1954), pp. 984-85, especially note 251 where further statistics are given.—EDITOR.]

[16] b. Berakoth 40a; b. Sanhedrin 70b. [English translations in *Seder Zera'im, Berakoth*, trans. Maurice Simon (London: Soncino Press, 1948), pp. 248-49, and *Seder Nezikin, Sanhedrin*, trans. H. Freedman, *Volume II* (1935), p. 478, in *The Babylonian Talmud*, ed. I. Epstein.—EDITOR.]

have dared to address God in this manner. Jesus did it always, in all his prayers which are handed down to us, with one single exception, the cry from the cross: "My God, my God, why hast thou forsaken me?" (Mark 15:34; Matt. 27:46); here the term of address for God was prescribed by the fact that Jesus was quoting Psalm 22:1. Jesus thus spoke with God as a child speaks with his father, simply, intimately, securely, childlike in manner. But his invocation of God as *abba* is not to be understood merely psychologically, as a step toward growing apprehension of God. Rather we learn from Matthew 11:27 that Jesus himself viewed this childlike form of address for God as the heart of that revelation which had been granted him by the Father. In this term *abba* the ultimate mystery of his mission and his authority is expressed. He, to whom the Father had granted full knowledge of God, had the messianic prerogative of addressing him with the familiar address of a child. This term *abba* is an *ipsissima vox*[17] of Jesus and contains *in nuce* his message and his claim to have been sent from the Father.

The final point, and the most astonishing of all, however, has yet to be mentioned: in the Lord's Prayer Jesus authorizes his disciples to repeat the word *abba* after him. He gives them a share in his sonship and empowers them, as his disciples, to speak with their heavenly Father in just such a familiar, trusting way as a child would with his father. Yes, he goes so far as to say that it is this new childlike relationship which first opens the doors to God's reign: "Truly, I say to you, unless you become like children again,[18] you will not find entrance into the kingdom of God" (Matt. 18:3). Children can say "*abba*"! Only he who, through Jesus, lets himself be given the childlike trust which resides in the word *abba* finds his way into the kingdom of God. This the apostle Paul also understood; he says twice that there is no surer sign or guarantee of the possession of the Holy Spirit and of the gift of sonship

[17] *Ipsissima vox* of Jesus = Jesus' own original way of speaking.

[18] As it might be translated from the Aramaic. The translation which is familiar to us remains possible: "unless you turn and become like children."

than this, that a man makes bold to repeat this one word, "Abba, dear Father" (Rom. 8:15; Gal. 4:6). Perhaps at this point we get some inkling why the use of the Lord's Prayer was not a commonplace in the early church and why it was spoken with such reverence and awe: "Make us worthy, O Lord, that we joyously and without presumption may make bold to invoke Thee, the heavenly God, as Father, and to say, Our Father."

The Two "Thou-Petitions"

The first words which the child says to his heavenly Father are, "Hallowed be thy name, Thy kingdom come." These two petitions are not only parallel in structure, but they also correspond to one another in content. They recall the *Qaddish* ("Holy"), an ancient Aramaic prayer which formed the conclusion of the service in the synagogue and with which Jesus was no doubt familiar from childhood. What is probably the oldest form of this prayer (later expanded) runs:

> Exalted and hallowed be his great name
>   in the world which he created according to his will.
> May he rule his kingdom
>   in your lifetime and in your days and in the lifetime
>   of the whole house of Israel, speedily and soon.
> And to this, say: amen.

It is from this connection with the *Qaddish* that we can explain the way in which the two "Thou-petitions" (in contrast with the two parallel "We-petitions") stand alongside each other without any connecting word; for in the earliest texts of the *Qaddish* the two petitions about the hallowing of the name and the coming of the kingdom appear not be connected by an "and."

Comparison with the *Qaddish* also shows that the two petitions are eschatological. They make entreaty for the revelation of God's eschatological kingdom. Every accession to power by an earthly ruler is accompanied by homage in words and gestures. So it will be when God enters upon his rule. Then

21

men will do homage to him, hallowing his name: "Holy, holy, holy, is the Lord God Almighty, who was and is and is to come" (Rev. 4:8); then they will all prostrate themselves at the feet of the King of kings, "We give thanks to thee, Lord God Almighty, who art and who wast, that thou hast taken thy great power and begun to reign" (Rev. 11:17). The two "Thou-petitions," to which in Matthew there is added yet a third one of like meaning ("Thy will be done, on earth as it is in heaven"), thus make entreaty for the final consummation. Their contents strike the same note as the prayer of the early church, *Maranatha* (I Cor. 16:22), "Come, Lord Jesus" (Rev. 22:20). They seek the hour in which God's profaned and misused name will be glorified and his reign revealed, in accordance with the promise, "I will vindicate the holiness of my great name, which has been profaned among the nations, and which you have profaned among them; and the nations will know that I am the Lord, says the Lord God, when through you I vindicate my holiness before their eyes" (Ezek. 36:23).

These petitions are a cry out of the depths of distress. Out of a world which is enslaved under the rule of evil and in which Christ and Antichrist are locked in conflict, Jesus' disciples, seemingly a prey of evil and death and Satan, lift their eyes to the Father and cry out for the revelation of God's glory. But at the same time these petitions are an expression of absolute certainty. He who prays thus, takes seriously God's promise, in spite of all the demonic powers, and puts himself completely in God's hands, with imperturbable trust: "Thou wilt complete Thy glorious work, *abba*, Father."

These are the same words which the Jewish community prays in the synagogue at the end of the service in the *Qaddish;* yet the two "Thou-petitions" are not the same as the *Qaddish,* in spite of the similar wording. There is a great difference. In the *Qaddish* the prayer is by a congregation which stands in the darkness of the present age and asks for the consummation. In the Lord's Prayer, though similar words are used, a congregation is praying which knows that the turning point has already come, because God has already begun his saving work. This congregation now makes supplication for full revelation of what has already been granted.

THE TWO "WE-PETITIONS"

The two "We-petitions," for daily bread and for forgiveness, hang together as closely as the two "Thou-petitions." This connection of the two "We-petitions" with one another is seen immediately in the structure through the fact that both of them, in contrast to the "Thou-petitions," consist of *two* half-lines each:

> Our bread for tomorrow / give us today.
> And forgive us our debts / as we also
> herewith forgive our debtors.

If it is correct that the two "Thou-petitions" recall the *Qaddish*, then we must conclude that in the Lord's Prayer the accent lies completely on the new material which Jesus added, that is, on the two "We-petitions." They form the real heart of the Lord's Prayer, to which the two "Thou-petitions" lead up.

(a) The first of the two "We-petitions" asks for daily bread (Greek, *ártos epioúsios*). The Greek word *epioúsios*, which Luther rendered as "täglich" ("daily") and Tyndale in 1525 and the King James Version as "daily," has been the object of lengthy discussion which is not yet finally settled. In my opinion, the decisive fact is that the church father Jerome (*ca.* A.D. 342–420) tells us that in the lost Aramaic *Gospel of the Nazarenes* the term *maḥar* appears, meaning "tomorrow," that here therefore the reference was to bread "for tomorrow." Now it is true that this *Gospel of the Nazarenes* is not older than our first three gospels; rather it rests on our Gospel of Matthew.[19] Nonetheless the Aramaic wording of the Lord's Prayer in the *Gospel of the Nazarenes* ("bread for tomorrow")

---

[19] [Cf. M. S. Enslin, "Nazarenes, Gospel of the," in the *Interpreter's Dictionary of the Bible* (New York: Abingdon, 1962), III, 524, who calls it an "Aramaic Targum" of our Gospel of Matthew and places it in the second century as a document.—EDITOR.]

must be older than the *Gospel of the Nazarenes* and older even
than our gospels. For in first-century Palestine the Lord's Prayer
was prayed in uninterrupted usage in Aramaic, and a person
translating the Gospel of Matthew into Aramaic naturally did
not translate the Lord's Prayer as he did the rest of the text.
Instead, when the translator came to Matthew 6:9-13, he of
course stopped translating; he simply wrote down the holy
words in the form in which he prayed them day by day. In
other words, the Aramaic-speaking Jewish–Christians, among
whom the Lord's Prayer lived on in its original Aramaic wording in unbroken usage since the days of Jesus, prayed, "Our
bread for tomorrow give us today."

Jerome tells us even more. He adds a remark telling how
the phrase "bread for tomorrow" was understood. He says:
"In the so-called Gospel according to the Hebrews[20] . . . I
found *maḥar*, which means 'for tomorrow,' so that the sense
is, 'Our bread for tomorrow—that is, our future bread—give us
today.' " [21] As a matter of fact, in late Judaism *maḥar*, "tomor-

[20] That is, the Gospel of the Nazarenes; see note 21.

[21] [Jerome, *Commentary on Matthew* on 6:11 and *Tract on Ps. cxxxv.*
The full Latin text is conveniently given in the notes (on Matt. 6:11) of
A. Huck–H. Lietzmann, *Synopse der Drei Ersten Evangelien* (Tübingen: J. C. B. Mohr, [10]1950), p. 30 (or in the corresponding English edition, ed. F. L. Cross, at the same passage): "In evangelio, quod appellatur
secundum Hebraeos, pro *supersubstantiali pane* reperi *maḥar*, quod
dicitur crastinum, ut sit sensus: panem nostrum crastinum, i.e., futurum,
da nobis hodie." The complete English translation of Jerome's comment
is provided in *Gospel Parallels*, ed. B. H. Throckmorton, Jr. (New York:
Nelson, 1949), in the notes on p. 25; or, together with all other excerpts
extant from the *Gospel of the Nazarenes*, in *The Apocryphal New Testament*, ed. M. R. James (Oxford: Clarendon Press, 1924), p. 4 (under
"The Gospel according to the Hebrews"); or now in *E. Hennecke: New
Testament Apocrypha*, ed. W. Schneemelcher, trans. R. McL. Wilson
and others (Philadelphia: Westminster, and London: Lutterworth),
Volume One: Gospels and Related Writings (1963), p. 147. It may be
noted that Jerome here speaks of "the so-called Gospel according to the
Hebrews," a title he regularly uses in one form or another, when, in
the opinion of many scholars today, he actually seems to be quoting
from an Aramaic *Gospel of the Nazarenes;* on this involved problem,
cf. Enslin, *op. cit.*, and *E. Hennecke: New Testament Apocrypha, op.
cit.*, I, 118-46, especially pp. 134 and 142, where views at odds with
Professor Jeremias' use of the material are also presented.—EDITOR.]

row," meant not only the next day but also the great Tomorrow, the final consummation. Accordingly, Jerome is saying, the "bread for tomorrow" was not meant as earthly bread but as the bread of life. Further, we know from the ancient translations of the Lord's Prayer, both in the East and in the West, that in the early church this eschatological understanding—"bread of the age of salvation," "bread of life," "heavenly manna"—was the familiar, if not the predominant interpretation of the phrase "bread for tomorrow." Since primeval times, the bread of life and the water of life have been symbols of paradise, an epitome of the fulness of all God's material and spiritual gifts. It is this bread—symbol, image, and fulfilment of the age of salvation—to which Jesus is referring when he says that in the consummation he will eat and drink with his disciples (Luke 22:30) and that he will gird himself and serve them at table (Luke 12:37) with the bread which has been broken and the cup which has been blessed (cf. Matt. 26:29). The eschatological thrust of all the other petitions in the Lord's Prayer speaks for the fact that the petition for bread has an eschatological sense too, i.e., that it entreats God for the bread of life.

This interpretation may perhaps be a surprise or even a disappointment for us. For so many people it is important that at least *one* petition in the Lord's Prayer should lead into everyday life, the petition for daily bread. Is that to be taken away from us? Isn't that an impoverishment? No, in reality, application of the petition about bread to the bread of life is a great enrichment. It would be a gross misunderstanding if one were to suppose that here there is a "spiritualizing," after the manner of Greek philosophy, and that there is a distinction made between "earthly" and "heavenly" bread. For Jesus, earthly bread and the bread of life are not antithetical. In the realm of God's kingship he viewed all earthly things as hallowed. His disciples belong to God's new age; they are snatched away from the age of death (Matt. 8:22). This fact manifests itself in their life down to the last details. It expresses itself in their words (Matt. 5:21-22, 33-37), in their looks (5:28), in the way they greet men on the street (5:47); it expresses itself also in their eating and drinking. For the disciples of Jesus there are no longer "clean" or "unclean" foods. "Nothing that a man eats can make him 'unclean'" (Mark 7:15); all that God provides is blessed. This "hallowing of life" is most clearly illustrated by the picture of Jesus at table for a meal. The bread which he proffered when he sat at table with publicans and sinners was everyday bread, and yet it was more: it was bread of life. The bread which he broke for his disciples at the Last Supper was earthly bread, and yet it was more: his body given for many in death, the gift of a portion in the atoning power of his death. Every meal his disciples had with him was a usual eating and drinking, and yet it was more: a meal of salvation, a messianic meal, image and anticipation of the meal at the consummation, because he was the master of the house. This remained true in the primitive church: their daily fellowship meals were the customary meals for sustenance, and yet at the same time they were a "Lord's supper" (I Cor. 11:20) which mediated fellowship with Him and linked in fellowship with one another those sitting at table (I Cor. 10:16-17). In the same way, for all his followers, every meal is a meal in his presence. He is the host who fills the hungry and thirsty with the fulness of his blessings.

It is in this sense too that the petition about "bread for tomorrow" is intended. It does not sever everyday life and the kingdom of God from one another, but it encompasses the totality of life. It embraces everything that Jesus' disciples need for body and soul. It includes "daily bread," but it does not content itself with that. It asks that amid the secularity of everyday life the powers and gifts of God's coming age might be active in all that Jesus' disciples do in word and deed. One can flatly say that this petition for the bread of life makes entreaty for the hallowing of everyday life.

Only when one has perceived that the petition asks for bread in the fullest sense, for the bread of life, does the antithesis between "for tomorrow" and "today" gain its full significance.

This word "today," which stands at the end of the petition, gets the real stress. In a world enslaved under Satan, in a world where God is remote, in a world of hunger and thirst, the disciples of Jesus dare to utter this word "today"—even now, even here, already on this day, give us the bread of life. Jesus grants to them, as the children of God, the privilege of stretching forth their hands to grasp the glory of the consummation, to fetch it down, to "believe it down," to pray it down—right into their poor lives, even now, even here, today.

(b) Even now—this is also the meaning of the petition for forgiveness, "And forgive us our debts as we also herewith forgive our debtors." This request looks toward the great reckoning which the world is approaching, the disclosure of God's majesty in the final judgment. Jesus' disciples know how they are involved in sin and debt; they know that only God's gracious forgiveness can save them from the wrath to come. But they ask not only for mercy in the hour of the last judgment—rather they ask, again, that God might grant them forgiveness already today. Through Jesus their lord, they, as his disciples, belong to the age of salvation. The age of the Messiah is an age of forgiveness. Forgiveness is the one great gift of this age. "Grant us, dear Father," they pray, "this one great gift of the Messiah's time, already in this day and in this place."

This second "We-petition" also has two parts, two half-lines, like the petition for daily bread. There is an antithesis, contrasting "Thou" and "we": "forgive us our debts as we forgive our debtors." The second half-line, about forgiving our debtors, makes a quite striking reference to human activity. Such a reference occurs only at this point in the Lord's Prayer, so that one can see from this fact how important this second clause was to Jesus. The word "as" (in "as we forgive") does not imply a comparison; how could Jesus' disciples compare their poor forgiving with God's mercy? Rather, the "as" implies a causal effect, for, as we have already seen (p. 14), the correct translation from the Aramaic must be, "as we also herewith forgive our debtors." With these words he who prays reminds himself of his own need to forgive. Jesus again and again declared this very point, that you cannot ask God for forgiveness if you are not prepared to forgive. God can forgive only if we are ready to forgive. "Whenever you stand praying, forgive, if you have anything against any one; so that your Father also who is in heaven may forgive you your trespasses" (Mark 11:25). At Matthew 5:23-24 Jesus even goes so far as to say that the disciple is to interrupt his presentation of the offering with which he is entreating God's forgiveness, if it occurs to him that his brother holds something against him; he is to be reconciled with his brother before he completes the offering of his sacrifice. In these verses Jesus means to say that the request for God's forgiveness is false and cannot be heard by God if the disciple has not on his part previously cleared up his relationship with the brother. This willingness to forgive is, so to speak, the hand which Jesus' disciples reach out toward God's forgiveness. They say, "O Lord, we indeed belong to the age of the Messiah, to the age of forgiveness, and we are ready to pass on to others the forgiveness which we receive. Now grant us, dear Father, the gift of the age of salvation, thy forgiveness. We stretch out our hands, forgive us our debts—even now, even here, already today."

Only when one observes that the two "We-petitions" are both directed toward the consummation and that they both implore its gifts for this present time, only then does the connection between the two "Thou-petitions" and the two "We-petitions" really become clear. The two "We-petitions" are the actualization of the "Thou-petitions." The "Thou-petitions" ask for the revelation of God's glory. The two "We-petitions" make bold to "pray down" this consummation, even here and even now.

The Conclusion: the Petition for Preservation

Up to this point, the petitions have been in parallel to one another, the two "Thou-petitions" as well as the two "We-petitions." Moreover the two "We-petitions" each consisted of two half-lines. Hence even the form makes the concluding petition, which consists of only a single line, stand out as abrupt and harsh:

> And let us not fall into temptation.

It also departs from the pattern of the previous petitions in that it is the only one formulated in the negative. But all that is intentional; as the contents show, this petition is supposed to stand out as harsh and abrupt.

Two preliminary remarks about the wording must be inserted, however. The first concerns the verb. The Greek text (literally, "and do not lead us into temptation") could be taken to imply that God himself tempts us. The Letter of James had already rigorously rejected this misunderstanding when—probably with direct reference to our petition—it said, "Let no one say when he is tempted, 'I am tempted by God'; for God cannot be tempted with evil and he himself tempts no one" (James 1:13). How the verb is really to be construed is shown by a very ancient Jewish evening prayer, which Jesus could have known and with which he perhaps makes a direct point of contact. The pertinent part (which recurs, incidentally, almost identically worded in the morning prayer) runs as follows:

> Lead my foot not into the power of sin,
> And bring me not into the power of iniquity,
> And not into the power of temptation,
> And not into the power of anything shameful.[22]

The juxtaposition of "sin," "iniquity," "temptation," and "anything shameful," as well as the expression "bring into the power of," show that this Jewish evening prayer has in view not an unmediated action of God but his permission which allows something to happen. (To put it in technical grammati-

---

[22] b. Berakoth 60b. [English translation in *Berakoth*, p. 378, *The Babylonian Talmud, op. cit.*; the morning prayer mentioned by Professor Jeremias, to be said as one washes his face, is given on p. 379.—EDITOR.]

cal terms: the causative forms which are here translated "lead" and "bring" have a permissive nuance.) The meaning therefore is, "Do not permit that I fall into the hands of sin, iniquity, temptation, and anything shameful." This evening prayer thus prays for preservation from succumbing in temptation. This is also the sense of the concluding petition of the Lord's Prayer. Hence we must render it, "Let us not succumb to temptation." That this reference in the final petition of the Lord's Prayer is indeed not to preservation *from* temptation but to preservation *in* temptation, is corroborated by an ancient extra-canonical saying of Jesus which, according to ancient tradition, Jesus spoke on that last evening, prior to the prayer in Gethsemane:

> No one can obtain the kingdom of heaven
> who has not passed through temptation.[23]

Here it is expressly stated that no disciple of Jesus will be spared testing through temptation; it is only the overcoming of temptation that is promised the disciple. This saying also testifies to the fact that the concluding petition of the Lord's Prayer does not request that he who prays might be spared temptation, but that God might help him to overcome it.

All this becomes fully clear when we ask, secondly, what the word "temptation" means. This word (*peirasmós* in Greek) does not mean the little temptations or testings of everyday life, but the final great Testing which stands at the door and will extend over the whole earth—the disclosure of the mystery of evil, the revelation of the Antichrist, the abomination of desolation (when Satan stands in God's place), the final persecution and testing of God's saints by pseudo-prophets and false saviors. The final trial at the end is— apostasy! Who can escape?

The concluding petition of the Lord's Prayer therefore says, "O Lord, preserve us from falling away, from apostasy." The

[23] [Cf. J. Jeremias, *Unknown Sayings of Jesus* (London: SPCK, and Greenwich, Connecticut: Seabury, 1957), pp. 56-59, for full details and discussion.—EDITOR.]

Matthean tradition also understood the petition in this way when it added the petition about final deliverance from the power of evil, which seeks to plunge men into eternal ruin: "But deliver us from evil."

Now, perhaps, we understand the abruptness of this last petition, why it is so brief and harsh. Jesus has summoned his disciples to ask for the consummation, when God's name will be hallowed and his kingdom come. What is more, he has encouraged them in their petitions to "pray down" the gifts of the age of salvation into their own poor lives, even here and now. But with the soberness which characterizes all his words, Jesus warns his disciples of the danger of false enthusiasm when he calls them abruptly back to the reality of their own threatened existence by means of this concluding petition. This final petition is a cry out of the depths of distress, a resounding call for aid from a man who in affliction prays:[24] "Dear Father, this one request grant us: preserve us from falling away from Thee." It is surely no accident that this concluding petition has no parallels in the Old Testament.

The doxology, "For thine is the kingdom and the power and the glory, for ever. Amen," is lacking completely in Luke, and in Matthew it is absent from the oldest manuscripts. We encounter it first in the *Didache*.[25] But it would be a completely erroneous conclusion to suppose that the Lord's Prayer was ever prayed without some closing words of praise to God; in Palestinian practice it was completely unthinkable that a prayer would end with the word "temptation." Now, in Judaism prayers were often concluded with a "seal," a sentence of praise freely formulated by the man who was praying.[26] This was doubtless also what Jesus intended with the Lord's Prayer, and what the congregation did in the earliest

[24] Cf. Heinz Schürmann, *Das Gebet des Herrn* (Freiburg: Herder, 1957), p. 90.

[25] *Supra*, pp. 3-4.

[26] Adolf Schlatter, *Der Evangelist Matthäus* (Stuttgart: Calwer Vereinsbuchhandlung, ⁵1959), p. 217.

period: conclude the Lord's Prayer with a "seal," i.e., a freely formulated doxology by the person praying. Afterwards, when the Lord's Prayer began to be used increasingly in the Service as a common prayer, it was felt necessary to establish a fixed formulation of the doxology.

If one ventures to summarize in *one* phrase the inexhaustible mystery of the few sentences in the Lord's Prayer, there is an expression pre-eminently suitable which New Testament research has especially busied itself with in recent decades. That phrase is "eschatology becoming actualized" [*sich realisierende Eschatologie*].[27] This expression denotes the age of salvation now being realized, the consummation bestowed in advance, the "in-breaking" of God's presence into our lives.

[27] ["Realized eschatology" was the phrase used, notably by C. H. Dodd, to describe the view that in the New Testament, and indeed already during Jesus' ministry, the new age had already fully come, toward which generations of prophets and seers had looked. But because this concept of "realized eschatology" does not do full justice to any future consummation (i.e., the New Testament hope for the Parousia or Second Coming), Professor Jeremias proposed the more comprehensive formula, *sich realisierende Eschatologie*—meaning that the decisive event came in Jesus Christ, but the full consummation lies in the future. Professor Dodd responded that he liked this German phrase but could not successfully put it into English (*The Interpretation of the Fourth Gospel* [Cambridge University Press, 1953], p. 447, note 1). Professor S. H. Hooke, in his translation of the first English edition of Professor Jeremias' book, *The Parables of Jesus* (London: SCM, and New York: Scribner, 1954), p. 159, used the phrase "an eschatology that is in process of realization," and this phrase has been widely employed. At least two problems are raised by such a rendering, however. (1) To some, "process" may suggest "progress" and even "evolution," a connotation quite foreign to the conceptual pattern which Professor Jeremias has in mind. The phrase might even call to mind misleading associations with "process philosophy." (2) The term "realization" can be ambiguous and suggest false connotations if it is given the sense equivalent to "illumination" or "understanding" (as in the sentence, "I came to a realization of the truth"). For these and other reasons, different phrases have been put forth to express the meaning of *sich realisierende Eschatologie*, including "inaugurated eschatology" (G. Florovsky) and "proleptic eschatology." Professor Jeremias himself prefers the translation suggested by Professor William Hull, of Southern Baptist Theological Seminary, Louisville: "eschatology becoming actualized."—EDITOR.]

Where men dare to pray in the name of Jesus to their heavenly Father with childlike trust, that he might reveal his glory and that he might grant to them already today and in this place the bread of life and the blotting out of sins, there in the midst of the constant threat of failure and apostasy is realized, already now, the kingly rule of God over the life of his children.

Clement of Alexandria has preserved a saying of Jesus which is not written in the gospels. It says, "Ask ye for the great things, so will God add to you the little things." [28] You are praying falsely, says the Lord. Always your prayers are moving in a circle around your own small "I," your own needs and troubles and desires. Ask for the great things—for God's almighty glory and kingdom, and that God's great gifts, the bread of life and the endless mercy of God, may be granted to you—even here, even now, already today. That does not mean that you may not bring your small personal needs before God, but they must not govern your prayer, for you are praying to your Father. He knows all. He knows what things his children have need of before they ask him, and he adds them to his great gifts. Jesus says: Ask ye for the great things, so God will grant you the little things. The Lord's Prayer teaches us how to ask for the great things.

[28] [Cf. J. Jeremias, *Unknown Sayings of Jesus, op. cit.*, pp. 87-89.— EDITOR.]

For Further Reading

By JOACHIM JEREMIAS

In the order mentioned in the Introduction:

The Parables of Jesus. London: SCM, and New York: Scribner's, 1954; rev. ed., 1963.

The Eucharistic Words of Jesus. Oxford: Basil Blackwell, and New York: Macmillan, 1955. Rev. ed., 1964.

Unknown Sayings of Jesus. London: SPCK, and Greenwich, Connecticut: Seabury, 1957.

Jesus' Promise to the Nations. ("Studies in Biblical Theology," No. 24.) London: SCM, and Naperville: Allenson, 1958.

Jerusalem zur Zeit Jesu. Göttingen: Vandenhoeck und Ruprecht, 1923-37; ²1958. Rev. ed., 1962.

Heiligengräber in Jesu Umwelt (Mt. 23, 29; Lk. 11, 47): Eine Untersuchung zur Volksreligion der Zeit Jesu. Göttingen: Vandenhoeck und Ruprecht, 1958.

Articles in the *Theologisches Wörterbuch zum Neuen Testament* (ed. Gerhard Kittel; Stuttgart: Kohlhammer), on the following terms and their derivatives:

Vol. I (1933)—"Abaddon," p. 4; "Abraham," pp. 7-9; *abyssos,* "abyss," p. 9; "Adam," pp. 141-43; "Hades," pp. 146-150; *airō,* "raise, bear," pp. 184-86; *amnos,* "lamb," pp. 342-45; *anthrōpos,* "man," pp. 365-67; "Armageddon," pp. 467-68; "Gehenna," pp. 655-56; *grammateus,* "scribe," pp. 740-42; and *gōnia, akrogōniaios, kephalē gōnias,* "cornerstone, keystone, head of the corner," pp. 792-93.

Vol. II (1935)—"Elijah," pp. 930-43.

Vol. III (1938)—*thyra,* "door," pp. 173-80; "Jeremiah," pp. 218-21; "Jonah," pp. 410-13; *kleis,* "key," pp. 743-53.

Vol. IV (1942)—*lithos,* "stone," pp. 272-83; "Moses," pp. 852-78; *nymphē,* "bride," pp. 1,092-99.

Vol. V (1954)—*pais theou* (with Walther Zimmerli), pp. 653-713 (English translation, *The Servant of God* ["Studies in Biblical Theology," No. 20; London: SCM, and Naperville: Allenson, 1957]); *paradeisos,* "paradise," pp. 763-71; *pascha,* "Passover, paschal," pp. 895-903.

Vol. VI (1959) — *poimēn,* "shepherd," pp. 484-501; *polloi,* "many," pp. 536-45; *pylē,* "gate," pp. 920-27; *"raka,"* pp. 973-76.

Vol. VII (in process)—"Samaria," pp. 88-94.

Also by Joachim Jeremias:

Infant Baptism in the First Four Centuries. London: SCM, and Philadelphia: Westminster, 1960. The other side of the question is presented in *Did the Early Church Baptize Infants?* by Kurt Aland (London: SCM, and Philadelphia: Westminster, 1963), to which, in turn, as a reply Professor Jeremias has written:

Nochmals: Die Anfänge der Kindertaufe. ("Theologische Existenz Heute," No. 101.) Munich: Christian Kaiser Verlag, 1962. English translation, *The Origins of Christian Baptism.* London: SCM, 1963.

The Sermon on the Mount. ("Facet Books, Biblical Series," No. 2.) Philadelphia: Fortress Press, 1963.

About the Lord's Prayer (literature especially cited by Professor Jeremias):

Fiebig, Paul. *Das Vaterunser.* Gütersloh: Bertelsmann, 1927.

Lohmeyer, Ernst. *Das Vater-unser.* Göttingen: Vandenhoeck und Ruprecht, 1946; [4]1960. Lohmeyer's remarks on the original Aramaic form are, on the whole, untenable.

Manson, T. W. "The Lord's Prayer," *Bulletin of the John Rylands Library, Manchester,* XXXVIII, Part 1 (Sept., 1955), 99-113, and Part 2 (March, 1956), 436-48.

Schürmann, Heinz. *Das Gebet des Herrn.* Freiburg: Herder, 1957.

For literature on the question of the original Aramaic form of the Lord's Prayer, see the titles cited by Professor Jeremias in note 12, above; to this list can be added:

Black, Matthew. *An Aramaic Approach to the Gospels and Acts.* Oxford: Clarendon Press, 1946, [2]1954.

Further literature on the Lord's Prayer mentioned in the Introduction:

On the Text

Metzger, Bruce M. "The Bodmer Papyrus of Luke and John," *The Expository Times,* LXXIII, No. 7 (April, 1962), 201-03.

Bammel, Ernst. "A New Text of the Lord's Prayer," *The Expository Times,* LXXIII, No. 2 (Nov., 1961), 54.

Word Studies

Jeremias, Joachim. "Abba," *Theologische Literaturzeitung,* LXXIX, No. 4 (April, 1954), cols. 213-14.

Metzger, Bruce M. "How Many Times Does 'Epiousios' Occur Outside the Lord's Prayer?" *The Expository Times,* LXIX, No. 2 (Nov., 1957), 52-54.

Hadidian, D. Y. "The Meaning of *epiousios* and the Codices Sergii," *New Testament Studies,* V, No. 1 (Oct., 1958), 75-81.

Liturgical Usage

Chase, Frederic Henry. *The Lord's Prayer in the Early Church.* "Texts and Studies: Contributions to Biblical and Patristic Literature," Vol. I, No. 3, ed. J. Armitage Robinson. Cambridge University Press, 1891.

Studies by Jewish Scholars

Abrahams, Isaac. *Studies in Pharisaism and the Gospels, Second Series.* Cambridge University Press, 1924. Pp. 94-108.
Montefiore, Claude G. *The Synoptic Gospels.* 3 vols.; London: Macmillan, 1909. See commentary on Matt. 6:9-13; Luke 11:2-4.

Other Studies

Hunter, A. M. *A Pattern for Life.* Philadelphia: Westminster, 1953. Pp. 64-74.
————. "The Lord's Prayer," in *Teaching and Preaching the New Testament.* Philadelphia: Westminster, 1963. Pp. 93-96.
Scott, E. F. *The Lord's Prayer: its Character, Purpose, and Interpretation.* New York: Scribner's, 1951.
Smith, C. W. F. "Lord's Prayer," in *The Interpreter's Dictionary of the Bible* (New York: Abingdon, 1962), III, 154-58.
George, A. Raymond. *Communion with God in the New Testament.* London: Epworth, 1953. Pp. 69-80.
Goulder, M. D. "The Composition of the Lord's Prayer," *The Journal of Theological Studies,* N. S., XIV, Part 1 (April, 1963), 32-45.

Facet Books

Titles already published:

Type used in this book
Body, 10 on 12 Janson
Display, Janson
Paper: White Spring Grove E. F.